A JAMESTOWN COLONY
TIME CAPSULE

ARTIFACTS OF THE EARLY AMERICAN COLONY

by Jessica Freeburg

Consultant:
Richard Bell, PhD
Associate Professor of History
University of Maryland, College Park

T0081119

CAPSTONE PRESS
a capstone imprint

Capstone Captivate is published by Capstone Press, an imprint of Capstone.
1710 Roe Crest Drive
North Mankato, Minnesota 56003
www.capstonepub.com

Library of Congress Cataloging-in-Publication Data is available on the Library of Congress website.
ISBN: 978-1-5435-9231-3 (library binding)
ISBN: 978-1-4966-6629-1 (paperback)
ISBN: 978-1-5435-9238-2 (eBook PDF)

Summary: What would you find in a time capsule of the Jamestown Colony? Perhaps a portrait of John Smith, glass beads, or a deer jawbone. Examine artifacts like these to explore the history of the first permanent English settlement in North America.

Image Credits
Alamy: Maurice Savage, 41; Getty Images: AFP/Brendan Smialowski, 30, Heritage Images/Fine Art Images, 34, Interim Archives, 33; iStockphoto: bauhaus1000, cover (top right), 14, milehightraveler, 42; Library of Congress: 27, 29, 38; National Geographic Image Collection: Ira Block, 18, 24, Robert Clark, 11, 16, 20, 32, Wood Ronsaville Harlin Inc., 17; Newscom: Album/British Library, 6, Glasshouse Images, cover (middle), 5; North Wind Picture Archives: 8, 12, 23, 36; Shutterstock: ale-kup (background), cover and throughout, Candus Camera, 21, Everett Historical, 25, 31, Joseph Sohm, 13, Kathy Clark, 43, stockphotofan1, cover (left); Wikimedia: National Portrait Gallery, London, 28

Editorial Credits
Editor: Julie Gassman; Designer: Lori Bye; Media Researcher: Svetlana Zhurkin; Production Specialist: Tori Abraham

Sensitivity Reader
Katrina Phillips, PhD, Assistant Professor of American Indian History, Macalester College, and member of the Red Cliff Band of Lake Superior Ojibwe

Table of Contents

CHAPTER 1

INTRODUCTION 4

CHAPTER 2

THE FIRST ENGLISH COLONISTS IN AMERICA . . . 6

CHAPTER 3

TENSIONS IN THE NEW WORLD 16

CHAPTER 4

THE STARVING TIME 20

CHAPTER 5

DAILY LIFE IN JAMESTOWN 24

CHAPTER 6

REDISCOVERING JAMESTOWN 38

More About the Artifacts 44
Glossary 46
Read More 47
Internet Sites 47
Index 48

Words in **bold** are in the glossary.

INTRODUCTION

When something important happens, we want to remember it. One of the ways we can do that is to save special things from that event. **Artifacts** such as maps, artwork, and buildings can be pieces of evidence that help to prove what happened. They can show how people reacted and remind us what was important about that moment in time. This collection of items could even be kept in a time capsule—a container of artifacts buried away for discovery in the future.

What if there were a special time capsule for each important moment in history? What if you found one of these time capsules? What might be in it?

Jamestown was named in honor of England's King James I.

In December 1606, 104 men and boys left London, England, to form a colony in North America. They docked their ships on the northeast bank of the James River, in present-day Virginia. Many of them would not survive the first year. But the homes, fort, and church they established would be the beginning of a new nation.

By examining an imaginary Jamestown time capsule, we can see how the first settlers lived and died. We can learn about the struggles they faced, and the triumphs that would eventually lead to the birth of the United States.

CHAPTER 2

THE FIRST ENGLISH COLONISTS IN AMERICA

From the Time Capsule:
MAP OF THE VIRGINIA COAST

If you opened the time capsule, you might see a roll of paper. Unrolling it might reveal a very old map of the Virginia coast. The map includes an island called Roanoke. This map was drawn by John White in 1585. White traveled from England to North America as part of an **expedition**. The group explored the area. England wanted to establish a colony there.

TIME CAPSULE
ARTIFACT:
MAP

In 1587, White returned to North America. He brought 113 colonists. The group planned to create a permanent home on Roanoke Island, in present-day North Carolina. They tried to form friendly relationships with the local Native nations. But living in an unfamiliar land was hard for the settlers. They didn't know how to grow food in the region. And things became tense between the colonists and some of the Natives.

The settlers needed supplies. And they needed more people to successfully establish their home in the New World. White returned to England to gather both. He left his family at the settlement. He planned to return soon.

Native Nations

Three large Native nations lived on the Virginia coast. They were there long before English explorers arrived. They were the Powhatan, the Monacan, and the Cherokee. There were many smaller groups within these larger nations. Each had their own chiefs and unique traditions.

John White searched for the lost colonists for nearly two months before returning to Europe.

However, a naval war between England and Spain delayed White's return to Roanoke. When he finally got back to the island, three years had passed. He saw no sign of the settlers. The only clue he found to what might have happened to them was the word *Croatoan* carved into a wooden post.

Croatoan was the name of an island near Roanoke. It was also the name of the Native nation living there. White hoped to find the missing colonists in that area. But a storm forced the crew to give up its search. White returned to England without finding the settlers. No sign of them was ever found. Their fate is one of the greatest unsolved mysteries in American history.

Fact

Virginia Dare was the first English child born in America. She was John White's granddaughter. She and her parents disappeared with the others from Roanoke.

From the Time Capsule: "YAMES TOWNE" CARGO TAG

Looking into the time capsule again, you might notice a small piece of metal. The words *Yames Towne* appear on it. You hold it in your hand. It's about the size of a large piece of bubble gum. Scientists believe the tag came to America in 1611. It likely arrived with supplies for the Jamestown colonists from London.

Twenty years after the Roanoke colony disappeared, 104 brave men and boys left England. It took four months for them to travel across the Atlantic Ocean. They arrived in America on May 14, 1607.

Creating a new English colony was their main goal. They also hoped to find gold. And they searched for a water route to the Pacific Ocean. Forming positive relationships with the Native Americans who already lived there was important. But they faced serious challenges.

TIME CAPSULE
ARTIFACT:
CARGO TAG

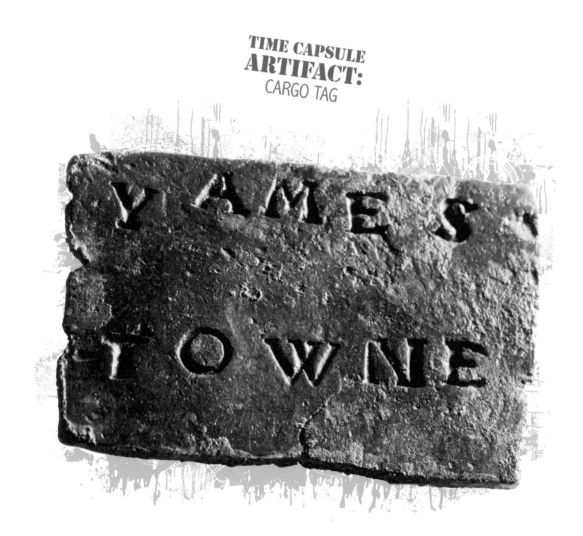

The water at the chosen site was deep, so ships could pull up close to land for easy unloading.

Growing food was difficult. The colonists were unfamiliar with the land. They had little knowledge about the crops that grew there. The region was also in the grip of a seven-year **drought**. Hunger and disease spread through the settlement. Many settlers died. Eight months after arriving, only 38 of the 104 original colonists survived.

The colonists relied on receiving supplies from England. The first ship with supplies arrived in January 1608. It also brought more colonists. Goods and settlers continued to come from England for many years.

Three Ships

The first settlers in Jamestown arrived on three ships. The *Susan Constant* was the largest. *Godspeed* was smaller. *Discovery* was the smallest. The *Susan Constant* and *Godspeed* returned to England. The *Discovery* was left behind for the men to use to explore the coast.

The three ships have been recreated and are part of Jamestown Settlement, a museum that tells the story of the colony.

TIME CAPSULE
ARTIFACT:
PORTRAIT

Returning your attention to the capsule, perhaps you see an engraved portrait of a man. He looks back at you with a strong gaze. The collar of his 1600s clothing sits high above his shoulders, framing a thick head of hair and full beard. This man was John Smith, an English explorer. He was an important member of the Jamestown community.

John Smith was Jamestown's first governor. Smith was a strict leader. He demanded that everyone do their share of work. His motto was, "He that will not work, shall not eat."

In 1609, Smith was injured in a mysterious gunpowder explosion. He sailed to England for treatment. He never returned to Virginia. But he is credited with creating some of the most detailed reports about the area during that time period.

CHAPTER 3

TENSIONS IN THE NEW WORLD

From the Time Capsule:
GLASS BEADS

TIME CAPSULE ARTIFACTS:
GLASS BEADS

Leaning over the time capsule to take a closer look, you might bump it. Something loose moves around in the container. You peer inside. Shiny beads roll among the other artifacts. They have holes through their centers. This allows them to be strung on a necklace or sewn onto fabric for decoration.

The colonists settled on a stretch of land that seemed to be empty. But the Powhatan people living nearby used the area for hunting and

gathering. Their leader, Wahunsenacawh, was known as Chief Powhatan. At first, he allowed his people to trade land and food with the English settlers. The colonists offered such things as metal tools, guns, and glass beads like those in the time capsule.

The Powhatan people grew corn and other crops.

Fact

Chief Powhatan's empire was extremely large. It covered 10,000 square miles (25,900 square kilometers) of land. That is roughly the size of the entire state of Massachusetts. It included almost 30 different tribes and 10,000 to 15,000 people.

From the Time Capsule:
PAINTED CERAMIC POTTERY

Perhaps you reach into the time capsule and touch the rough edges of a broken clay pot. Containers like these were used by the Powhatans and other Native people to hold food. They also used pots like this to trade food with the English colonists for other goods.

TIME CAPSULE
ARTIFACT:
CERAMIC POT

Chief Powhatan was a wise leader. He negotiated with John Smith. The chief allowed the colonists to share hunting grounds with his people. The chief's daughter, Pocahontas, is believed to have been around 11 years old when the English arrived. Written accounts note that Pocahontas often went with other Powhatan people to deliver food to Jamestown. She was reportedly seen playing with the English children.

A Priest's Prediction

Around the time the colonists arrived, one of Powhatan's priests predicted that a nation would arise from the Chesapeake Bay and destroy Chief Powhatan's empire. The English had arrived in that area. Still, Powhatan thought the threat to his empire would come from the Native nations his people had been fighting with for many years. Sadly, the Powhatan Indians were eventually forced from most of their land by the English colonists. As more colonists arrived in Virginia, they expanded their claim on the land, often with violence.

CHAPTER 4

THE STARVING TIME

From the Time Capsule:
DEER JAWBONE AND CORNCOBS

TIME CAPSULE
ARTIFACTS:
JAWBONE AND CORNCOBS

If you continued to sift through the time capsule, you might feel the smooth edge of a jawbone. You run your fingers across the row of teeth still rooted into the bone. Beside it, you might see several blackened corncobs. You let your hands feel the bumpy surface.

The colonists depended on corn grown by Natives to survive.

The colonists learned how to grow and eat foods they could harvest locally. They hunted and roasted deer and wild turkey. They traded such things as guns, metal tools, hatchets, and glass beads for corn.

By the fall of 1609, approximately 350 men, women, and children called Jamestown home. But a severe seven-year drought limited the food supply for both the Natives and the colonists. The Powhatan Indians stopped trading food with the settlers.

A series of conflicts led to the beginning of four years of fighting. This was known as the first Anglo-Powhatan War. Desperate to eat, the colonists began taking food by force. In turn, the Powhatan Indians began killing any English settler who went outside the fort. Colonists were confined to the fort. They no longer had access to fresh water and were unable to go into the woods to hunt.

The colonists ate whatever animals they could find in the fort. First, they ate all the dogs, cats, and horses. As they became more desperate, they ate rats, venomous snakes, and even the leather from their shoes.

From the autumn of 1609 to March 1610, 80 percent of the colonists at Jamestown died from starvation or violence.

Colonists suffered from diseases caused by lack of healthy food and fresh drinking water. Many died from starvation and illnesses like dysentery, typhoid, and scurvy. Those who survived hoped a supply ship coming from England would arrive soon. But a hurricane stranded the ship in Bermuda for 10 months. The ship arrived in Jamestown in late May 1610. By then, only 60 colonists were still alive.

Fact

George Percy was the governor of Jamestown during the Starving Time. He reported that colonists dug up the graves of their fallen friends and resorted to **cannibalism** to survive.

CHAPTER 5

DAILY LIFE IN JAMESTOWN

From the Time Capsule:
TOBACCO PIPES

As you continue looking through the time capsule, a funnel-shaped piece of clay mixed with bits of broken pottery might catch your eye. You pick up the funnel-shaped object. You run your fingers across a thin stem that grows into a rounded bowl on the other side. This tobacco pipe was discovered by **archaeologists** in Jamestown. Tobacco was an important part of the livelihood of those who lived in Jamestown.

TIME CAPSULE
ARTIFACTS:
PIPE PIECES

Before John Rolfe started growing tobacco,
the colonists tried to make money other ways,
including producing glass, silk, and lumber.

In the summer of 1610, England sent more colonists
and supplies to Jamestown. The colony rebuilt. But for
Jamestown to survive, the colonists needed something
they could sell to people in England.

John Rolfe brought the answer to Jamestown
on a supply ship in 1612. He had tobacco seeds with
a unique flavor that would become the preferred
tobacco in England. The colonists finally had a
commodity they could sell.

In 1613, Chief Powhatan's daughter, Pocahontas, now around 17 years old, was kidnapped by the colonists. They hoped to use her to arrange a trade for colonists who had been taken as prisoners. Her capture led to the end of the first Anglo-Powhatan War.

While she was in captivity, Pocahontas met John Rolfe. Rolfe was 10 years older than she was. There are no records of Pocahontas's feelings or thoughts, but colonists' records suggest the two fell in love. After Pocahontas **converted** to Christianity, she and Rolfe were married in 1614 with her father's blessing. The marriage brought several years of peace between the colonists and the Powhatan people. During this time, the Virginia region became a top producer of tobacco.

The marriage between Pocahontas and John Rolfe is believed to be the first recorded marriage between a Native American and a European.

As you look back into the time capsule, you could see a sheet of paper with the image of a woman on it. This is the only known portrait created of Pocahontas. It was engraved while she was in England. She was thought to be 21 years old when she posed for this portrait.

During her trip to England, Pocahontas was considered a princess and treated with respect.

Pocahontas and Rolfe had one child—a son named Thomas. While the family visited England, her portrait was drawn. The couple attended social events, such as balls and plays. She even met the royal family. Sadly, as her family prepared to travel back to Virginia, Pocahontas became ill. She passed away in March 1617, before she could return to America.

EXCAVATION SITE OF ANGELA HOUSE

Reaching into the time capsule again, maybe you run your hand across the rough surface of a red brick. This brick was excavated from the site that is called the Angela Site. The site is the former home of Captain William Pierce.

TIME CAPSULE ARTIFACTS: BRICKS

Pierce was a wealthy planter and merchant who lived in Jamestown. He purchased a woman named Angela in 1619 when the first Africans were brought to the New World. Angela was one of more than 20 people purchased and enslaved by the colonists at that time.

Angela was the first African woman to be documented in the Virginia **census**. Little is known about her. Records indicate she was kidnapped from her home in southern Africa. Then she was forced to travel to America aboard a slave ship called the *Treasurer*. More than 100 of the captives on board during the journey to America died from disease and the ship's terrible conditions. Archaeologists are **excavating** the home that Angela lived in. They hope to learn more about her and her daily life.

When the first Africans arrived in Jamestown, it was the start of more than 240 years of slavery in North America.

From the Time Capsule:
QUARTZ ARROWHEAD

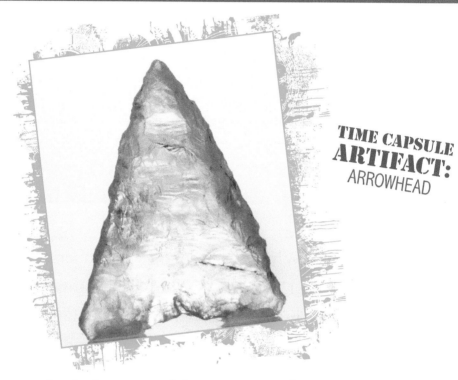

TIME CAPSULE
ARTIFACT:
ARROWHEAD

At the bottom of the time capsule you could find a smooth stone triangle. Although it is only a couple of inches tall, arrowheads like these were tiny killers. They helped the Powhatans hunt wildlife for food. The Powhatans also used arrows to defend their hunting and gathering grounds against the settlers. The colonists were taking more land to grow and harvest tobacco.

Opechancanough struck his axe against a cabin's walls in anger during negotiations with the colonists.

When Chief Powhatan passed away in 1618, his brother Opechancanough became chief. The Natives and colonists continued living in relative peace for several more years. But more settlers arrived from England. The English expanded their settlement. The Powhatan people lost more and more of their land. Chief Opechancanough became increasingly angry.

About a quarter of the English colonists died in the fighting on March 22, 1622.

On the morning of March 22, 1622, the Powhatans began moving onto the plantations. The English colonists living outside Jamestown had little reason for concern. The settlers and Powhatan Indians had lived peacefully side by side for eight years. But the warriors had orders from Opechancanough to attack swiftly and without warning. They killed 347 settlers. The colonists in Jamestown were warned by a Native. That warning allowed them to save themselves.

Reinforcements arrived from England and declared war against the Powhatan. The second Anglo-Powhatan War lasted from 1622 to 1632. When an English captain went to a Powhatan village for peace talks, he and his men poisoned the drink used to toast the peace **treaty**. Two hundred Powhatans died from the poison. The English shot and killed another 50 Powhatans who survived the poisoning.

The third Anglo-Powhatan War began in 1644 when the Powhatan Indians attacked the settlers. Between 400 and 500 colonists were killed. Two years later, the English and Powhatan signed the Treaty of 1646. It gave the king of England control over the Powhatan tribes. It also allowed the English to settle in areas the Native people had formerly occupied. The treaty restricted where the tribes could live.

English forces captured Chief Opechancanough in 1646.

In 1677, the Powhatan signed the Treaty of Middle Plantation, agreeing to give annual **tribute** payments of fish and game to the English. This tradition continues today. Symbolic tributes are given in honor of the history between the Virginia Natives and the colonists.

Seventy years after the colonists first arrived in Virginia, the vision the priest shared with Chief Powhatan came true. A nation from the Chesapeake Bay destroyed the chief's empire. The Native people who once lived freely throughout the area found themselves with just a small **reservation** to call their own.

CHAPTER 6

REDISCOVERING JAMESTOWN

From the Time Capsule:
CHURCH TOWER PHOTOGRAPH

TIME CAPSULE
ARTIFACT:
PHOTOGRAPH

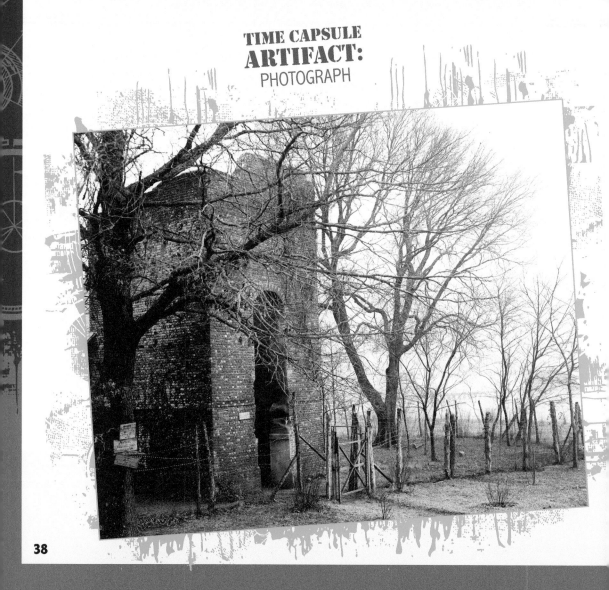

If you inspected the time capsule again, a black-and-white photograph might catch your eye. You pick it up, careful not to let your fingers smudge the image, and look at it more closely. A crumbling brick tower surrounded by leafless trees fills the space. This tower, decayed by time and weather, was once at the heart of Jamestown. In this image, it stands alone.

After the treaties were signed, the colonists had more land on which to settle. They lived on plantations that would become new colonies. Jamestown became the capital of Virginia. It remained the center of the developing colonies until the capital moved to Williamsburg in 1699. Slowly, Jamestown began crumbling and faded into the wildlife surrounding it.

For decades, many thought this tower was the only surviving piece of Jamestown. The area around it was overgrown with trees. Some believed most of the settlement was lost beneath the rising water of the James River. They were wrong.

Families picnicked in the shade of the crumbling tower. They didn't realize they were sitting on top of the remains of England's first successful colony in North America. Old wells that once supplied the colonists with water were now filled in and hidden under the forest.

When archaeologists began digging, they were surprised and delighted by what they found. These items were hidden for hundreds of years. They told scientists more than they'd ever known before about what life was like for those brave settlers.

TIME CAPSULE
ARTIFACT:
HAT

Perhaps the final artifact you find in your time capsule is a beige hat. You run your fingers over the frayed thread around the brim. This hat was once worn by a member of the **Confederate** Army during the Civil War.

The Civil War took place between 1861 and 1865. The area that had once been Jamestown was used for a Confederate fort during that time. By 1893, the land surrounding the crumbling church tower was privately owned. The owners donated it to an organization dedicated to preserving the history of Virginia.

Today, Jamestown's church tower is much closer to the water than it was in the 1600s.

Archaeologist William Kelso believed the church tower was located in the middle of the settlement. This meant much of the land Jamestown once occupied was above water. Excavation began on April 4, 1994.

The Jamestown Rediscovery archaeological project has found and preserved more than 2 million artifacts. We can now better understand how the earliest English settlers lived and died as they adjusted to life in a strange new world.

Today, visitors can tour the site. Archaeologists continue to dig up artifacts from the original colony. In the Jamestown Settlement historical park, visitors can see replicas of the boats that carried the first colonists to America and reproductions of settlers' homes. There is also a Powhatan village. Costumed historical actors allow visitors to step back in time.

Jamestown Settlement features Powhatan hut replicas.

More About the Artifacts

Map of the Virginia Coast

This engraving by Theodor de Bry was published in a book called *America, Volume I,* in 1590. It was based on a map created by colonist John White. White drew it during an expedition to Roanoke Island.

"Yames Towne" Cargo Tag

Archaeologists found this tag at the bottom of a well in Jamestown. It traveled on NASA's Space Shuttle Atlantis in 2007. They wanted to honor the explorers who created the first permanent English settlement.

Portrait of John Smith

John Smith kept journals of his experiences in New England while living in Jamestown. These journals were published in 1612. They offered residents of Great Britain a glimpse into the New World. As a result, many made the journey across the Atlantic Ocean in hope of a better life.

Glass Beads

These beads from 1607 were discovered during the excavation of Jamestown. This excavation began in 1994 and continues today.

Painted Ceramic Pottery

Thirty-seven thousand pieces of pottery handmade by the Powhatans between 1607 and 1610 have been found during the excavation of Jamestown.

Deer Jawbone and Corncobs

The colonists learned to hunt local wildlife such as deer and turkey. They traded with the Natives to obtain corn. These food sources soon became a main part of their diet. The discovery of these items during the excavation of Jamestown is a reminder of how the colonists adapted to their new agricultural surroundings.

Tobacco Pipes

Smoking tobacco in a pipe was a very common practice in the 1600s. It was particularly popular in Europe. The colonists could use the tobacco they grew to help their community survive. They sold their tobacco crops to buyers in England.

Engraving of Pocahontas

Although there are many images depicting Pocahontas, this is the only portrait made of her during her short life. The Virginia Company likely had the portrait done to showcase the refined daughter of a powerful Native leader and to help encourage more English families to move to the New World.

Excavation Site of Angela House

Archaeologists excavated the property where Angela lived and served the Pierce family. They hope to learn more about her life by examining the items they found. Actors portray Angela during special programs at Historic Jamestowne. This helps visitors understand what it might have been like for those who were enslaved and brought to an unfamiliar world.

Quartz Arrowhead

Virginia's Native nations made arrowheads out of a variety of materials ranging from stone and bone to wood. Stone arrowheads were the type of arrowhead most commonly found in Jamestown by archaeologists. It's believed that many of the arrowheads recovered from Jamestown came there through trade rather than through warfare.

Church Tower Photograph

This tower was added to the fourth church that was built in Jamestown after the third church was burned down during a rebellion in 1676–1677. It had a bell housed in the upper floor under a wooden roof. It was abandoned in the 1750s. It remained standing for hundreds of years, the only above ground structure remaining of the first permanent English colony in America.

Confederate Army Hat

Confederate soldiers built a fort around the crumbling church tower during the Civil War. In 1862, the Confederates abandoned the fort when they were forced to retreat. Union soldiers and black Americans who had once been enslaved lived there until the end of the war in 1865.

Glossary

archaeologist (ahr-kee-OL-uh-jist)—specialist who studies prehistoric people, cultures, and artifacts

artifact (AHR-tuh-fakt)—object such as a tool or pottery made by humans during an earlier time that typically tells modern society something about the past

cannibalism (KA-nuh-buhl-izm)—the practice of eating the flesh of another person

census (SEN-suhs)—an official count of all the people living in a country or district

commodity (kuh-MOD-i-tee)—a product with value that can be used for trade or commerce

Confederate (kuhn-FE-der-uht)—referring to a person who supported the South during the Civil War

convert (kuhn-VURT)—to leave behind a previous religion or beliefs and adopt a new religion or set of beliefs

drought (DROUT)—an extended period of time without rainfall that leaves an area struggling to grow crops

excavate (EKS-kuh-vayt)—to dig in the earth to search for ancient remains or ruins

expedition (ek-spi-DISH-uhn)—a journey made for the purpose of exploration

reservation (rez-er-VAY-shuhn)—an area of land set aside by the U.S. government for Native nations

treaty (TREE-tee)—an official agreement between two or more groups or countries

tribute (TRIB-yoot)—a payment made by one ruler or nation to another to obtain peace or protection

Read More

Lüsted, Marcia Amidon. *The Jamestown Colony Disaster: A Cause and Effect Investigation.* Minneapolis, MN: Lerner Publications, 2017.

McAneney, Caitie. *Uncovering the Jamestown Colony.* New York: Gareth Stevens Publishing, 2017.

Rusick, Jessica. *Living in the Jamestown Colony: A This or That Debate.* Mankato, MN: Capstone Press, 2020.

Internet Sites

Jamestown Rediscovery: Historic Jamestowne
https://historicjamestowne.org

Colonial America: Jamestown Settlement
https://www.ducksters.com/history/colonial_america/jamestown_settlement.php

National Geographic Kids: On the Trail of Captain John Smith
https://kids.nationalgeographic.com/games/adventure/on-the-trail-of-captain-john-smith-old/

Index

African Americans, 30–31
Angela Site, 30, 31, 45
Angela (slave), 30–31, 45
Anglo-Powhatan Wars, 22, 26, 35–36
archaeology, 24, 30, 31, 40, 42, 43, 44, 45
arrowheads, 32, 45

beads, 16, 17, 21, 44

cannibalism, 23
capital city, 39
cargo tag, 10, 44
census, 31
Cherokee people, 7
church tower, 39–40, 41–42, 45
Civil War, 41, 45
Confederate Army, 41, 45

Dare, Virginia, 9
de Bry, Theodor, 44
Discovery ship, 13
diseases, 12, 23, 31
drought, 12, 21

excavations, 30, 31, 42, 44, 45
expeditions, 6, 44

food, 7, 12, 17, 18, 19, 21, 22–23, 32, 44

Godspeed ship, 13
gold, 10

hunting, 17, 19, 21, 22, 32, 44

James River, 5, 40
Jamestown Rediscovery project, 42–43
Jamestown Settlement historical park, 43

Kelso, William, 42

map, 6, 44
Monacan people, 7

Opechancanough (chief), 33, 34

Percy, George, 23
Pierce, William, 30, 45
pipe, 24, 44
Pocahontas, 19, 26, 28–29, 45
poisoning, 35
pottery, 18, 44
Powhatan (chief), 17, 19, 26, 33, 37
Powhatan people, 7, 17, 18, 19, 21–22, 26,
      32–37, 43, 44, 45
preservation, 41–43

Roanoke colony, 6, 7, 8, 9
Rolfe, John, 25, 26, 29
Rolfe, Thomas, 29

ships, 5, 12, 13, 23, 25, 31
slavery, 30–31, 45
Smith, John, 15, 19, 44
Susan Constant ship, 13

tobacco, 24, 25, 26, 32, 44
trade, 17, 18–19, 21, 44, 45
Treasurer ship, 31
Treaty of 1646, 36
Treaty of Middle Plantation (1677), 37
tribute payments, 37

White, John, 6–9, 44
Williamsburg, Virginia, 39